The Home Foreclosure E-Book: Tried and True Methods to Save Homes in Foreclosure

Table of Contents

Introduction	Pg. 3
Foreclosure Process Overview	Pg. 9
Defining a Mortgage	Pg. 12
Chances Are Your Foreclosure Could Be Wrongful	Pg. 16
Three Reasons Why You Should Care About Home Foreclosure	
Improper Mortgage Securitization:	Pg. 19
Identifying Mortgage Assignment Fraud:	
Six Action Steps	Pg. 21
Challenging A Mortgage (Before Foreclosure)	Pg. 23
How to Fight Foreclosure (After the Sale)	Pg. 26
9 Proven Steps to Prevent Home Foreclosure	Pg. 27
More Resources	Pg. 34

Disclaimer: This information is not intended for legal advice, nor does it provide direct legal advice. The use of this e-book is for educational and informational purposes only.

© Copyright and Trademark of Ultisky Inc. 2013 all content and rights reserved. The materials herein are being provided for informational and educational purposes only and intended for one purchase use and may not be reproduced.

About The Author

Kyle Martin Ransom is an American entrepreneur who was also a U.S. Navy War Veteran under Top Secret Clearance. Ransom serves as the CEO of Ultisky, Inc. specialized in providing online publishing, mobile publishing, and e-commerce. He is a seasoned financial industry expert and a former mortgage broker with over 16 years of experience. Ransom was also a real estate investor and developer. Kyle, has a strong passion for music and implementing music projects.

Introduction

Hi let me introduce myself, my name is Kyle Ransom creator of the **Go Fight Foreclosure System.** I have been involved in many aspects of real estate as a real estate investor and developer, mortgage loan officer and mortgage broker for a total of sixteen years of experience. I have fought and beat foreclosure on my own investment properties when I could not move them when banks were deflating home values and I could not sell my properties.

The key to fighting foreclosure is learning how to identify wrongful actions taken by the LENDERS to plan your foreclosure defense!

The foreclosure crisis still continues to affect millions of homeowners today with no end in sight. It is expected that there will be another five million foreclosures processed before this crisis finally comes to an end.

One out of three homeowners is facing foreclosure, in default or knows a homeowner in foreclosure! Let's face it the foreclosure crisis is very bad.

This book will address the foreclosure process and explain how you can protect you and your home from foreclosure.

About Government Support or Lack of It

The US government has tried to remedy this crisis by passing bills to help curve the many foreclosures across the nation. They even started allocating funds to buy and fix up foreclosed homes, urging lenders to offer loan modifications and guaranteeing the loans in case they go back into default. *However the bills that have been passed have only helped very few homeowners in default or in foreclosure. The vast majority of the loan modifications that were processed really did not offer much support since most of the loan modifications that were processed did not reduce the monthly mortgage payments enough to make them affordable and in many cases increased the monthly mortgage payment thus making it even less affordable.*

The truth is because there are so many people trying to work out a loan modification lenders just do not have the manpower to process all of the requests. Another reason is that many lenders have their hands tied because they have to answer to their investors and many investors are NOT willing to take a cut on their returns to grant a loan modification.

So the bottom line is that while it may be perceived that there are many options, there are really NOT a whole lot of options effective to prevent foreclosures. There are just too many foreclosures out there for all of them to be handled effectively.

The only way to ensure that YOU as a homeowner protect yourself from foreclosure is to become more proactive and educated about the foreclosure process and use that knowledge to your advantage. In fact more than ever it is essential for you to become more proactive. Why you ask? Well, the reason why WHAT lenders don't want YOU to know. The industry's dirty little secrets MUST be exposed.

You see back before when the real estate market was booming and record numbers of mortgages were processed as a result of the booming economy there was also huge amounts of mortgage portfolios that were **packaged** and ==resold== to what was called the secondary market.

This was common practice for mortgage loan companies and banks to do this so that they could free up money to do more loans. They were extremely greedy, very greedy. It did NOT matter if the loan was bad or good, which MOST of these loans were really bad deals for the homeowners.

The Problem:

==**Here is the thing; a vast majority of those loan portfolios were sold off without proper documentation**==. Many of these portfolios were sold many times and owned at the SAME time by different holders plus many of the companies are now out of business. Therefore many lenders do not have proper documentation to show true ownership of the debt.

So it is highly likely many foreclosures that are being conducted today are NOT even legal.

==**The key to fighting foreclosure is learning how to identify wrongful actions taken by the LENDERS to plan your foreclosure defense!**==

Sadly though, thousands upon thousands of lenders STILL conduct illegal foreclosures.

How is this possible?

Quite simply those homeowners did not know that they have the right to contest their foreclosures. As a result, their homes were foreclosed or I should say stolen from them. Think about it. If someone you don't know came to you and said hey, you own me $5,000 pay me now, wouldn't YOU want some type of proof that you owed them? I know I would.

It is the same thing here when a foreclosure notice is issued by "ANY" bank or mortgage servicer representing the BANK.

The bank is basically saying "Hey you owe me X amount of dollars so pay me now or I plan to foreclose and take your home." There is nothing in a foreclosure notice to prove that your lender has the right to foreclose. After all, there is no copy of the assignment of the note or anything else for that matter showing that they rightfully own the note to collect the debt in Due Course!

The lender is so certain that you will accept the fact that you are in foreclosure and won't challenge their rights to foreclose on your home. After all you probably hadn't made any payments in at least three months right? So they really can come take the house, right?

What homeowners are failing to realize is that even though you are late on your mortgage payments whatever lender issues you have the foreclosure notice does not mean they have the granted right to foreclose.

But they will foreclose ONLY if the homeowner does not contest the foreclosure.

It is up to homeowners to take action immediately once a foreclosure notice is issued.

How is that done you ask? Well that depends on where the foreclosure is taking place and whether or not if the foreclosure is in a judicial state.

In Judicial states, <u>the bank must prove</u> that the mortgagor is in default. Once the bank has exhausted its attempts to resolve the default with the homeowner they then contact an attorney to pursue court order to foreclose.

The attorney contacts the homeowner to attempt to resolve the mortgage default. If the homeowner is unable to pay off the default, the attorney usually files a lis pendens (order pending) with the court. The lis pendens gives notice to the public that a pending action has been filed against the homeowner. The purpose of the order is to provide proof of a default and get the court's approval to begin foreclosure.

In a non-judicial state foreclosures are started with a deed of trust that contains a power of sale clause. The clause facilitates the trustee to initiate a mortgage foreclosure sale, without ever having to go to court.

The trustee is required to issue a notice of default and notify the homeowner. If the homeowner does not respond, the trustee may then initiate a foreclosure sale. To challenge a non-judicial foreclosure the homeowner will need to start a lawsuit against the mortgage lender.

So requesting that the lender produce the original mortgage note will also require that homeowners put protection in place to prevent the foreclosure while fighting the lawsuit.

More and more homeowners have realized that they must take matters into their own hands in order to effectively fight foreclosure to get a better deal. This technique is probably the most effective to do because it puts the legal burden on the lender to perform or else. You have to force the lender to give you a better deal.

For the first time ever, homeowners now have strong legal defenses to go up against their lenders and win.

There are many cases already that have exposed many lenders who have tried to illegally foreclose on homeowners across the nation because the lender was not able to show that they owned the debt and therefore could not foreclose.

Because of this growing trend, more and more lenders are being exposed for their questionable business practices when foreclosing on homeowners they knowingly put in bad loans.

Here are some points you may want to consider when putting together a defense strategy to fight foreclosure on your home.

You can further research these points by checking your state foreclosure laws (many states passed laws that are more in favor of homeowners facing foreclosure).

Uniform Commercial Code

Uniform Commercial Code is a valuable resource to fight foreclosure (**http://www.law.cornell.edu/ucc/ucc.table.html**).

In order for a foreclosure to be legal the debt holder must first show that they actually own the debt. Usually it is required that the lender provides the original note in order to satisfy the courts.

However, some lenders have gotten away with providing a certified copy of the note, which by law does not legally show that they own the note. If a judge allows a certified copy of the note challenge that this is NOT authentic!

Sometimes you may have to take your case to a higher court to get justice. File an appeal if you feel that you did NOT get justice. Fight the foreclosure to the end.

Own the Mortgage Note in Due Course.

Let me explain, remember when I said earlier that loans were sold off in bulk without proper documentation. What I meant by that was when the loan portfolios were sold an assignment was supposed to be recorded and attached to the note and security to show the note and deeds were transferred from the sale.

This was supposed to be done at every sale. Now remember when I also said the loan portfolios were often sold many times over and OVER and even sold to different holders at the SAME time plus many of the companies are NOW out of business.

In reality most of these assignments were NEVER recorded at the time of sale (no securitization) and in most ALL cases a loan has been sold more than twice or even five to ten times.

In most cases, the lender claiming to be the holder of the mortgage note in due course authorized to foreclose on your home has a problem. In other words, they must SHOW how they got the mortgage note in the chain of title. Assignments must transfer in ORDER from lender A, B, and C etc.

Missing Intervening Mortgage Assignments

If the foreclosure was allowed to proceed with missing intervening mortgage assignments, you as the homeowner would be At Risk of owing the SAME debt again.

Uniform Commercial Code has special defenses to protect YOU to fight foreclosure in this example.

RESPA Violations

Other defense strategies to consider when fighting your lender for a better deal are RESPA violations (common with sub-prime loans) ,predatory lending practices (again common with sub-prime loans, low income homeowners and minorities) inflated homes values, misleading loan officers and brokers (mostly fall under RESPA violations).

Federal Reserve Defense – Case of John Daly You can also use the Federal Reserve angle. In a nutshell, the argument here is that since the banking system is based on a fractional reserve system, a system that allows banking companies to create money out of debt, the lender did NOT in fact own the money that they lent out and therefore do not have to the right to foreclose.

You can learn more on this defense by reading the booklet published by the Chicago Bank entitled Modern Money Mechanics. You can also watch a video on the subject.

Http://video.google.com/videoplay?docid=7065205277695921912.

The video is more than an hour long but you get to learn more about the fractional reserve system in the first thirty minutes of the video. Also the video touches on the infamous case of John Daly who fought his lender against foreclosure and won using this defense argument.

I hope this E-book will enlighten you and empowers you with the knowledge to act, become more proactive and educated so that you too can fight your foreclosure effectively.

Foreclosure Process Overview

What is Foreclosure?

Foreclosure typically involves a lawsuit to which a bank, mortgage lender, or other creditor seeks to take a property back that was secured for a debt. The bank or lender can take the property back or request that the property is sold to pay off the debt. The foreclosure results in the homeowner losing whatever rights they had in the property. The homeowner will no longer be the owner of the property.

Important Key Terms

Default— a mortgage is considered in default when more than one payment is due and is unpaid. The mortgage is generally due on the 1st of each month. Most banks allow a 15-day grace period.

Delinquent Payment— a mortgage payment that is not made by the day it is due.

Equity— The value of the property deducted from what you still owed on the property.

Forbearance— Typically a written or oral agreement to repay the delinquency of a loan over a period of time.

Important Tips

Federally insured mortgages, such as FHA, HUD, or VA, are granted special rights under foreclosure protection. FHA, HUD, or VA mortgages may extend the period before foreclosure, award moderate repayment plans or even allow for the government agency to buy out the lender.

You will need to contact the mortgage lender to find out what options are available if you have a federally insured mortgage.

It is very helpful to understand that foreclosure processes and laws vary from state to state.

Judicial Foreclosure

The bank must prove that the mortgagor is in default. Once the bank has exhausted its attempts to resolve the default with the homeowner they then contact an attorney to pursue court order. The attorney contacts the homeowner to attempt to resolve the mortgage default. If the homeowner is unable to pay off the default, the attorney files a lis pendens (order pending) with the court. The lis pendens gives notice to the public that a pending action has been filed against the homeowner. The purpose of the order is to provide proof of a default and get the court's approval to begin foreclosure.

Explaining lis pendens: Filed by a lender, a lis pendens is the formal notice that starts the foreclosure process in a judicial foreclosure state.

Non-judicial Foreclosure

Non-judicial foreclosures are started with a deed of trust that contains a power of sale clause. The clause facilitates the trustee to initiate a mortgage foreclosure sale, without ever having to go to court. The trustee is required to issue a notice of default and notify the homeowner. If the homeowner does not respond, the trustee may then initiate a foreclosure sale.

Foreclosure Laws by States – Some States do both Judicial and Non- Judicial

State	Judicial	Non-Judicial	State	Judicial	Non-Judicial
Alabama	•	•	**Montana**	•	
Alaska		•	**Nebraska**	•	
Arizona	•	•	**Nevada**		•
Arkansas	•		**New Hampshire**		•
California		•	**New Jersey**	•	
Colorado		•	**New Mexico**	•	
Connecticut	•		**New York**	•	
Delaware	•		**North Carolina**		•
Dist. of Col.		•	**North Dakota**	•	
Florida	•		**Ohio**	•	
Georgia		•	**Oklahoma**	•	
Hawaii		•	**Oregon**		•
Idaho		•	**Pennsylvania**	•	
Illinois	•		**Rhode Island**		•
Indiana	•		**South Carolina**	•	
Iowa	•		**South Dakota**	•	•
Kansas	•		**Tennessee**		•
Kentucky	•		**Texas**		•
Louisiana	•		**Utah**	•	
Maine		•	**Vermont**	•	
Maryland	•	•	**Virginia**		•
Massachusetts		•	**Washington**	•	•

Michigan   •   •   West Virginia   •
Minnesota   •   Wisconsin   •
Mississippi   •   **Wyoming**   •
Missouri   •

Defining a Mortgage

Firstly, a mortgage by itself is not considered a debt. However, a mortgage is most often used as evidence that a debt exist. A mortgage is used as a security pledge of property to a mortgage lender, which is most often used to secure a mortgage loan. The interest in the property or land is transferred to the mortgage lender to secure the mortgage loan. The interest of ownership is returned when terms of the mortgage agreement have been fulfilled.

A mortgage is security for a mortgage lender who finances a mortgage loan and becomes the Mortgagee (legal term). Mortgage lenders seek to protect their interest and the mortgage secures the mortgage loan to take precedence over additional creditors. This allows the mortgage lender to register the mortgage against the title of the property. The borrower of the mortgage debt will be discharged once it is paid off and if the debt is not paid off the Mortgagee reserves the right to foreclose against the borrower.

The mortgage lender is identified as the Mortgagee and the borrower is identified as the Mortgagor.

Common Types of Mortgages

Mortgage Loans	Loan Breakdown	Borrowers Defined
Fixed rate mortgage (30,20,15,10 years)	• Interest rate & monthly payment remain the same for the entire term of the loan	• plan to live in property more than 10 years • like total payment stability
10/1 year adjustable rate mortgage	• Interest rate & monthly payment remain the same for 10 years Starting the 11th year, interest rate adjusted every year, so payment is subject to change every year for remainder of loan	OR • plan to live in property more than 10 years • like initial payment stability, can accept later changes • plan to move within 10 years • want loan to remain in force in case plans change
7/23 (2-Step)	• Interest rate &	• plan to live in property

or '30 due in 7' mortgage	monthly payment remain the same for 7 years Conversion option: On the 8th year, interest rate adjusted to reflect prevailing interest rates, resulting payment will remain the same for remainder of loan	more than 10 years • can tolerate one payment adjustment **OR** • plan to move within 7 years • want to remain in force in case plans change
7/1 year adjustable rate mortgage	• Interest rate & monthly payment remain the same for 7 years Starting the 8th year, interest rate adjusted every year, so payment is subject to change every year for remainder of the loan	• plan to live in property more than 7 years • like initial payment stability, can accept later changes **OR** • plan to move within 7 years • want loan to remain in force in case plans change
7 year ballon mortgage	• Interest rate & monthly payment remain the same for 7 years • At the end of 7 years, loan is due in full. Borrower must refinance into new loan at prevailing interest rates	• plan to live in property more than 7 years • are willing to refinance at prevailing market rates **OR** • plan to move within 7 years • like payment stability
5/25 (2-Step) or	• Interest rate & monthly payment	• plan to live in property more than 5 years

13

'30 due in 5' mortgage	• remain the same for 5 years Conversion option: On the 6th year, interest rate adjusted to reflect prevailing interest rates, resulting payment will remain the same for remainder of loan	• can tolerate one payment adjustment **OR** • plan to move within 5 years • want loan to remain in force in case of plans change
5/5 & 5/1 year adjustable rate mortgages	• Interest rate & monthly payment remain the same for 5 years Starting the 6th year, interest rate adjusted every 5 years (for 5/5 ARM) and every year (for 5/1 ARM)	• plan to live in property more than 5 years • like initial payment stability, can accept later changes **OR** • plan to move within 5 years • want loan to remain in force in case plans change
5 year balloon mortgage	• Interest rate & monthly payment remain the same for 5 years At the end of 5 years, loan is due in full. Borrower must refinance into new loan at prevailing interest rates	• plan to live in property more than 5 years • are willing to refinance at prevailing market rates **OR** • plan to move within 5 years
3/3 & 3/1 year adjustable rate mortgages	• Interest rate & monthly payment remain the same for 3	• like payment stability • plan to live in property more than 3 years • like initial payment

	years Starting 4th year, interest rate adjusted every 3 years (for 3/3 ARM) and every year (for 3/1 ARM)	stability, can accept later changes
	OR	• plan to move within 3 years
		• want loan to remain in force in case plans change
1 year adjustable rate mortgages	• Interest rate adjusted every year, so monthly payment is subject to change every year for entire 30 year loan term	• want to take advantage of lowest rate possible
		• are willing to accept yearly payment changes
	OR	
		• cannot qualify at higher rate programs

Source: Interest.com

Chances Are Your Foreclosure Could Be Wrongful

Foreclosures are spreading all across America and many homeowners are giving up their American dream because they don't know how to fight back. Some homeowners give up without ever even putting up a fight. This is a huge mistake as there is a growing trend of more and more lenders being exposed conducting unlawful foreclosures on thousands of homeowners. As a result, these mortgage companies are ordered to stop foreclosures and pay out large sums of money for damages. Odds are in your favor that your lender may be conducting a wrongful foreclosure on your home. If you have received a foreclosure notice or you are at risk of losing your home to foreclosure, now is the time to evaluate your mortgage.

How to evaluate your mortgage and see if your lender may be wrongfully foreclosing on your home? Certainly, the mortgage lender is NOT going to tell you if they have done wrong by you. However, you can train yourself how to look for solutions to challenge your lender and possibly save your American dream.

Receiving a Default Notice:

Once your mortgage goes into default you will receive a notice from your mortgage lender that your mortgage is behind and you will have an opportunity to cure the default. The lender will notify you by certified mail when they plan to foreclose and give you an opportunity to dispute the foreclosure. This is your golden opportunity to fight to stop foreclosure and possibly keep your home. Often during this time homeowners facing foreclosure simply give up and usually most walk away.

Time is YOUR Worst Enemy:

You will need to act fast! The mortgage lender hires a foreclosure attorney to handle these proceedings for them. Generally, you will need to supply an Answer back to the foreclosure attorney and file it with the courts if you want to fight your foreclosure. You can answer your claim or hire an attorney to assist you. However, foreclosure laws vary from state to state and this guide will provide information how to handle fighting foreclosure according to what foreclosure procedure your State follows.

If you believe that your mortgage company did not act in your best interest, fight to keep your property! Once you receive notice of foreclosure you usually have about 20 days from the date of the notice to dispute the debt. It is crucial that you answer the foreclosure notice within that 20-day period.

Today, many homeowners are evaluating their mortgages and challenging their mortgage lenders for misrepresentation and winning!

It is NOT okay if your mortgage lender allowed an inflated appraisal. If you don't challenge the mortgage lender and seek damages for their actions they win and you lose.

Did your mortgage lender quote you one interest rate and make you believe differently than what you actually got? If you don't challenge the mortgage lender and seek damages for their actions they win and you lose.

Have you reviewed your loan documents and found that your mortgage lender received access lender fees? If you don't challenge the mortgage lender and seek damages for their actions they win and you lose.

If your mortgage lender cannot prove that they own the note or cannot show how they got control of the note through a sales transaction and you don't challenge the mortgage lender they win and you lose. I think you get the picture.

Foreclosure Authority

Your mortgage lender does not want you to know that they lack standing to foreclose on your home. That is especially if your loan was written before 2010.

Here is why....

When you closed on your loan the lender had options of how your documents would be stored and recorded. To save on money and a gold rush to write as many loans as they could possibly do they stored documents in the electronic registry of MERS (Mortgage Electronic Registration Systems, Inc). therefore, skipping paying a recording fee at the county courthouse and using the system of MERS.

This greed caused improper mortgage securitization of your loan. It effected who would be the proper Holder In Due Course for your loan and causing clouds on title so the any transfers of that loan would also have clouds in the chain of title.

For this very reason the majority of properties are not true clear and marketable titles free from liens. The lenders know this so when they sell a bank owned property they request that the purchaser sign a hold harmless wavier. Investor could care less because the victim that had their home stolen and wrongfully foreclosed on is not likely going to claim any interest in the property later on down the road.

Secrets Inside The $25 Billion Settlement

Just like in the famous game of Monopoly the BIG banks will have a chance pass. You know if a chance comes to use a get out of jail FREE card when a homeowner says you committed mortgage fraud with Robo signing to foreclose on my house. It should make you disgusted to think that forged documents and affidavits are being used in court cases to illegally foreclose on homeowners.

And by the way, it is STILL happening today! The Government settlement that will likely include ALL 50 states in the end is giving the big bankers a license to commit fraud. All those in favor of the $26 Billion Dollar sell out settlement here are some facts to consider before you drink the Kool-Aid just yet.

1. Crime should be punishable!

If you do the crime you should do the time. That means **JAIL** time for criminal illegal activity.

2. $25 or $26 Billion vs. $500 Billion

The settlement of $26 Billion is TOO LOW! Should be $500 Billion or more in my opinion! "The $26 Billion will only help a select few and not really. You see over 11 million people face foreclosures. Only 1 million will be helped and they are still not the lucky ones." Write downs on mortgages will be $20,000. Sorry, but just ask any realtor who will tell you that the average homeowner is much more upside down than $20K! A setup for the homeowner to fail to carry a mortgage with no equity and making payments they still cannot afford.

Those who will receive financial compensation will be given $1,500 to $2,000 if they are lucky. One of my family members got a whopping $500 for the big banks wrong doing! That does not even cover the deposit and first month's rent on an apartment these days.

3. Foreclosure mills get more aggressive!

YES! The foreclosure attorneys are not concerned about being notified of wrong doings for example, warning that robo-signers exist on the security instrument assignments. Why would they ever care about the bank not having enforceable security interest now that this <u>Get Out Of Jail FREE Card</u> is able to be used by chance.

Three Reasons Why You Should Care About Home Foreclosure Improper Mortgage Securitization

Most people really don't understand a lot about mortgages and home foreclosure. Actually, the majority of homeowners no matter what background or education have very little knowledge about the terms of their mortgage note. All the average homeowner knows is that closing on the mortgage allowed them to purchase their dream home. Which is good enough for most to understand.

What if the economy went bad and you got laid off? Worst what if you got sick and had no means to earn a living? The worst of the evils what if both happened to you? Well, this is the story of most people facing foreclosure today in America and even around the world.

The first option is always to see what you can work out with the bank. Like say a simple loan modification until you get back on your feet? Typically, banks are unwilling to give help to unemployed homeowners despite what you hear in the media.

Reacting To a Foreclosure Notice

Before the bank forecloses on a property the homeowner has the best negotiating position. This is the prime time to get the bank to reduce principal balance and interest rates on a mortgage loan. A solution to work out a loan modification that is more affordable considering the true value the home is worth right now.

Improper Mortgage Securitization

Detecting improper mortgage securitization is a saving grace to stopping foreclosure. Using this home foreclosure defense is the best solution to get the bank to work with you. Typically, the majority of mortgage loans in danger of foreclosure have securitization flaws. However, most homeowners don't know when mortgage securitization is improper.

When conducting your research on your mortgage it's a very good idea to do a title search on your property. The title search will show all of the transactions that took place on your property including mortgage assignments or lack of. A title search can be done at the county clerk's office or online. You can also hire a title examiner. What you are looking for is whether or not the assignment was properly filed. In most cases they are not. This is very common with third parties company such as (MERS)

What is a Mortgage Assignment?

This is a written document serving as evidence of a transfer of a loan obligation from the original borrower to a third party. It reveals that a mortgage has been transferred the deed of trust or security deed is the debt attached to the mortgage that is now owed to the new owner.

This is where research and discovery is most critical when stopping home foreclosure. A mortgage assignment transfers the rights of the original lender to a new holder. Keep in mind, the original lender is Paid OFF. So the new holder must prove to be in Possession of the original mortgage note and a holder in due course if challenged to have a legal standing to foreclose.

Identifying Mortgage Assignment Fraud: Six Action Steps

Action 1 – Identify the date the mortgage assignment was executed and recorded. Generally, the mortgage assignment will be executed soon before the foreclosure sale date. How is it possible that the mortgage assignment is valid and the owner is truly a holder in due course?

Action 2 – Did MERS (Mortgage Electronic Registration Systems, Inc) serve as Nominee? MERS is a separate corporation and is often the beneficiary of over 50 million loans held in securitized trusts. However, MERS assignments purports that it transfers the mortgage note which would be the deed of trust in non-judicial states or security deed in Georgia (all known as the debt) but also includes the transfer of the Note.

Note: would be the deed of trust in non-judicial states or security deed in Georgia (all known as the debt) but also includes the transfer of the Note. Note That MERS has NO Authority to Transfer the NOTE.

Action 3 – Does the mortgage assignment have a corporate seal affixed? It may be challenged that it is not valid if it does not.

Action 4 – Review all signatures and look up the notary name and examine the signature on the mortgage assignment. Now research the notary name on file in the state that the notary is registered. Review the signature of the notary on file and it should match your mortgage assignment. However, the recorded mortgage assignment will likely have a notary signature that are Squiggle Marks (OMG !!) hard to make out an actual signature name.

It can be challenged that the notary signature do not match and that the document is invalid. Here is where it gets interesting, typically, ALL of the signatures on your mortgage assignment are Squiggle Marks !! But you can clearly see that ALL the signatures on your mortgage assignment are squiggle marks. Why are the signatures squiggle marks? Well, if MERS is involved which this is usually the case they will assign MERS "Authorized Signators" who are employees of its member institutions that are located throughout the country and these "Authorized Signators" routinely execute Assignments even though they are NOT employed by MERS. This makes the foreclosure process easier for them.

This allows them to execute the mortgage assignment and have it recorded just days before a foreclosure lawsuit is filed or a trustee's sale takes place.

Action 5 – Review the signing officers on the mortgage assignment and it can be challenged that, how can someone assign my mortgage for a company that they don't even work for solely for the purpose of foreclosing on my home particularly right before getting ready to foreclose on me? What is the problem? This fraudulent act completely circumvents proper laws that govern how to document the Chain of Assignment and Ownership. Hence who is the TRUE "Holder In Due Course"?

Action 6 – Do you have a Pretender Lender? Generally, MERS is hiding or NOT Listed. This is often a successor in interest to a mortgage company no longer in business or that purchased your mortgage company.

Challenging a Mortgage (Before Foreclosure)

Most mortgage loans were pooled into what is known as investor funded securitization trusts. The mortgage lender collecting payments are typically servicing companies assuming responsibility for collecting payments on behalf of the securitized loans of former banks that are no longer even in business. Typically, when you are notified that you should start making payments to a new mortgage lender, if that new lender is not the original mortgage note holder of interest and the new lender <u>should have</u> proper documentation to be able to collect payments and especially foreclosing on a property.

A problem facing many mortgage lenders acting as servicing companies is that they cannot produce mortgage notes. This means that often these servicing companies have no proof of ownership and no provable rights to foreclose or collect monthly mortgage payments.

If a mortgage lender cannot produce an original mortgage note, their right to foreclosure on a property is not validated as the Mortgagee (<u>Mortgage Lender</u>). Often servicing companies are foreclosing by attempting to substitute original mortgage notes with a copy. There must be a "Count to Establish Lost Documents," which is strict requirements. The servicing company will have to prove that they actually own the property with no evidence of an original mortgage note. ANYONE can stake this exact same claim. This is no easy task for mortgage lenders acting as servicing companies. It is highly likely that if the mortgage note was sold and transferred that the current note holder will not be able to validate true ownership of the note and homeowners facing foreclosures are using this method to challenge their foreclosures.

Here Are Some Effective Ways to Challenge Mortgage Lenders Before The Foreclosure Sale:

<u>Make Them Produce The Note</u>

The mortgage lender is forced to validate true ownership of the note by providing the original note to the courts. Here in odds are in the homeowner's favor because chances are the mortgage lender does not have the original note especially if it was sold or transferred. Many mortgage lenders have tried and failed to counter this by requesting that a certified copy be allowed to be used to validate true ownership of the note. However some have succeeded in states where judges are less sympathetic to homeowners in foreclosure.

<u>Make Them Show Due Course</u>

Just as the mortgage lender must produce the original note document, the mortgage lender must also show how they took ownership of the note. When mortgage notes are sold the transaction must be recorded on title in order to show that mortgage lender has control of the mortgage note in due course. This can be a good defense if the mortgage notes that were sold multiple times as most mortgage notes are.

Predatory Lending Practices

Mortgage with high interest rates or questionable mortgage terms can be considered predatory lending. Predatory Lending Practices have been very common with sub-prime mortgages and mortgage offered to the poor and uneducated homeowner. Many unethical mortgage companies would write loans to homeowners knowing that they really couldn't afford it. These lending practices were considered to be what caused the foreclosure crisis in the first place. However the truth has been exposed and the real cause of the foreclosure crisis was **GREED**.

Predatory Lending Case Study

Mr. and Mrs. Clark found out through researching their mortgage documents that fraudulent and predatory lending practices were involved. The appraisal was showing a highly inflated value of $120,000 and misrepresented i.e. it was stated that a mobile home was part of the property when actually it wasn't and that their house wasn't on a septic tank when it was.

Also the mortgage company originated a very high interest rate loan that Mr. and Mrs. Clark really could not afford. This lending practice is very common with elderly homeowners. As a result the loan was originated based on the inflated value of $120,000 at an interest rate of 9.5%.

They forced their mortgage lender to stop the foreclosure and negotiate a loan modification therefore reducing the mortgage payment from $1,200 per month to $500 a month!

Fraudulent Lending Practices

This is a great way to challenge a mortgage lender if there are any issues with the appraisal, or the loan documents. A common example of fraudulent loan practices would be an appraisal that has been greatly inflated in order to qualify a loan or increase the amount of fees to be charged. When a homeowner was not properly informed or even purposely deceived in order the get the homeowner to sign off on a bad loan. Or loan documents are signed by ROBO-signers who in fact do not really represent the lender. There were many instances of this type of lending practices during the Sub-Prime mortgage boom. For sub-prime mortgage holders this may be a good way to challenge mortgage lender.

Truth in Lending Act (TILA) Foreclosure Defense

A federal statute was put into place by the Truth in Lending Act (TILA) to protect borrowers and consumers against unscrupulous and dishonest lenders. This statute allows borrowers to be able to compare rates between lenders and requires that lenders be honest in disclosing all the details of a loan.

TILA Violations:

The act requires that lenders have to make certain disclosures known to the borrowers especially before they sign loan documents. The following must be disclosed:

1. Amount of the loan and payment amounts
2. Any Prepayment penalties
3. Late charges and due dates
4. APR (Annual Percentage Rate) for the mortgage
5. Application or service fees

A violation of the TILA results in the lender being forced to cancel the deed of trust against the property. This prevents the lender from being able to foreclose. All TILA violations must be discovered within three years from the time the loan was closed.

<u>If you discover a TILA violation within one year you may even be entitled to seek damages and recover your credit if it is discovered within one year.</u>

A Common Easy TILA violation to spot: Check loan documents to see if the lender failed to write in an expiration date of your "notice of right to cancel" on the loan document.

Whatever the situation may be the ultimate goal is to get the mortgage company to offer you a better deal! This is an excellent time to establish loan modifications, reduce fees, interest rates, etc. Fight the mortgage company to give you a payment plan deal that you can really afford or at the very least get your foreclosure proceedings stopped.

How to Fight Foreclosure After The Sale

Homeowners can still contest the foreclosure even after the foreclosure sale has taken place. Actually, this could put the homeowner at a greater advantage if the foreclosure was indeed a wrongful foreclosure. The reason being is that the lender has completed the foreclosure even though they really did not have the legal right to do so and could expose the lender to even more liability.

This can offer great leverage when filing a case against the lender. In fact, several major lenders have been ordered to pay compensation to homeowners who did lose their homes to wrongful foreclosure.

Once the foreclosure sale is completed the lender will start eviction proceedings. So therefore, it will be necessary to file suit to stop eviction proceedings while the case is pending. One way to do that is to request a temporary and permanent injunction. Once filed all eviction proceedings will cease until the injunction is ruled upon in court.

9 Proven Steps to Prevent Home Foreclosure

Step 1: Foreclosure Notice

\# Non Judicial State

If you live in a non-judicial state it is not necessary for the mortgage lender claiming enforceable security interest to get court approval to foreclose.

\# Judicial State

In a judicial state the mortgage lender claiming enforceable security interest must seek court approval before the foreclosure can take place.

#•Some States Allow Non-Judicial and Judicial Foreclosures How-to determine what type of foreclosure is being used? -If the mortgage lender filed a lawsuit against you which requires that you provide an "Answer" to the foreclosure complaint this is known as a judicial foreclosure.

-Should you receive a Notice of Foreclosure informing you of a specific date and time that your home will be sold at a public auction under power this is known as a non-judicial foreclosure.

Refer to the Foreclosure Laws of your state, the lender foreclosing must follow these laws specifically.

Step 2: Foreclosure Authority

#• Identify the party attempting to foreclose on the property. This is the party claiming enforceable security interest.

#• Is the party foreclosing on the property the original lender? #•You can determine this information by looking through the original closing documents.

#• Examine the Promissory Note and Security Instrument.

#•The Promissory Note is the NOTE often referred to as Note, Interest First Note, Adjustable Rate Rider Note, etc. It will be title as Note somewhere in the document. This is the contract that establishes the terms and conditions for payments.

#•The Security Instrument is what binds the debt to be owed on the NOTE. Which is why the party claiming enforceable security interest will always foreclose on the Security Instrument.

#•A Security Instrument is referred to as a Deed Of Trust, Mortgage, or Security Deed. The party claiming enforceable security interest will be foreclosing on the Security Instrument.

#•Often the Security Instrument has been transferred by Assignment to another party. Mortgage Electronic Registration Systems, Inc. also known as MERS is a third party separate entity that alleges to act as nominee for the original lender to transfer Assignments of Security Instruments.

Step 3: Foreclosure Defense

#•Establish who is claiming enforceable security interest which grants the authority to foreclose on the property.

-Is it the original lender foreclosing on the property? Foreclosure Defense Against Original Lender -If it is the original lender foreclosing on the property the original lender must be a Holder In Due Course. The only way for a party to claim enforceable security interest is to be a Holder In Due Course under UCC Uniform Commercial Code.

#•An original lender who is foreclosing must also foreclose on the Security Instrument even if the original lender is in possession of the original Note.

#• Important: The Promissory Note and Security Instrument must have been kept together at all times by the original lender.

#•Did the original lender enter the Security Instrument into Mortgage Electronic Registration Systems, Inc. registry?

#•Examine the Security Instrument it will reveal if Mortgage Electronic Registration Systems, Inc. is the nominee for the original lender. This means the Security Instrument is registered in the registry of Mortgage Electronic

Registration Systems, Inc. opposes to being recorded in county records together with Promissory Note and Security Instrument held together.

#•Should the original lender give the Security Instrument to ANY party separating the Security Instrument from the Promissory Note the authority to foreclose is not valid. To bind the debt of the Security Instrument for the Promissory Note the documents are inseparable they must be held together.

#•Any Assignment transfer of the Promissory Note and Security Instrument must be transferred together. Even the original lender must be transferred a Promissory Note and Security Instrument together.

#•The original lender must also have expressly written permission in the Promissory Note for the Note to be transferred to ANY party and that includes even to itself because the Promissory Note and Security Instrument can never be separated.

Step 4: Foreclosure Defense from New Lender By Assignment Transfer

#•Review the Assignment Transfer of the Security Instrument to determine who is assigning the Security Instrument to the new lender to claim enforceable security interest.

#•The Assignment Transfer is referred to as an Assignment of Deed of Trust, Assignment of Mortgage, or Assignment Of Security Deed. Often it can be a Corporate Assignment as well.

#•Examine the Promissory Note. Look for instructions in the Promissory Note that states that it can be transferred by another party. If it does not state that the Promissory Note can be transferred by another party it can never be transferable by another party.

-Even if an original lender is assigning the Promissory Note it still must be together with the Security Instrument because the two documents are inseparable. They must be held together at all times.

#•Important: The Assignment transfer of the Security Instrument must state to transfer the Promissory Note and Security Instrument together. Further, to make the Assignment transfer valid the Promissory Note must specify that permission is given to another party to transfer the Note.

#•Assignment transfers are invalid that do no transfer the Promissory Note and Security Instrument together.

#•Assignment transfers are invalid that only transfer the Security Instrument.

#•Assignment transfers are invalid that do not have permission from the original lender in the Promissory Note to transfer the Note.

Step 5: Foreclosure Defense from MERS

#•The best foreclosure defense from Mortgage Electronic Registration Systems, Inc. is to apply the strategy of theory and research.

#•Is Mortgage Electronic Registration Systems, Inc. acting as nominee and separate entity?

#•Once it is established that MERS is acting as nominee and separate entity which is generally the case. It is now important to build a defense against MERS authority to transfer the Note to any party.

#•Examine the promissory note this is the contract of how payments will be made and to. The payments are set up to be made to the lender. Only the lender can grant express permission to MERS or any other party to transfer the promissory note.

#•If the lender never granted permission in the promissory note contract to transfer the note it should never be transferred. This is the biggest defense against MERS! They never had permission to in the promissory note to transfer the note to any party.

Reference Note:

The promissory note and security instrument are two separate documents which must remain together. This is also upheld by the Supreme Court. Because MERS never owned title to the security instrument placing it in MERS registry system and separating the security instrument from the promissory note is invalid. This is improper mortgage securitization violation 101. Generally, MERS is hardly ever the beneficiary. However, sometimes MERS can be named the beneficiary.

Refer to Carpenter v. Longan, 83 U.S. (16 Wall) 271, 274 (1872).

The note and mortgage are inseparable; the former as essential, the latter as an incident. An assignment of the note carries the mortgage with it, while an assignment of the latter alone is a nullity.

The biggest argument that makes MERS in the chain of title improper is that MERS never held title to note.

In order for the lender to foreclose they must foreclose on the security instrument when MERS is involved.

Creating MERS was an electronic system short cut for recording documents. When a homeowner misses payments on a mortgage loan the foreclosure process is started using the foreclosure law in the state the home is located.

When a judicial foreclosure is started it requires the lender to seek court approval to foreclose on the homeowner. In this matter the homeowner is allowed to Answer and dispute the lender's claim to foreclose on the property.

A non-judicial foreclosure requires no court approval for the lender to foreclose on the home. As such the homeowner typically must sue the lender to dispute the foreclosure.

Disputing MERS Foreclosure

Most often the promissory note was documented in BLANK.

Like showing "Pay to the order of _____, without recourse". Refer to U.S. BANK NATIONAL ASSOCIATION vs. Antonio IBANEZ. "A blank assignment was not acceptable proof of perfection of title for the promissory note. "

<u>Step 6: Qualified Written Request to Stop Foreclosure</u>

A Qualified Written Request or (QWR) was created because various companies associated with the buying and selling of real estate, such as lenders, real estate agents, construction companies and title insurance companies were often engaging in providing undisclosed kickbacks to each other, inflating the costs of real estate transactions and obscuring price competition by facilitating bait-and-switch tactics. For example, a lender advertising a home loan might have advertised the loan with a 5% interest rate, but then when one applies for the loan one is told that one must use the lender's affiliated title insurance company and pay $5,000 for the service, whereas the normal rate is $1,000. The title company would then have paid $4,000 to the lender. This was made illegal. The reason is to make prices for the services clear so as to allow price competition by consumer demand and to thereby drive down prices.

The Act prohibits kickbacks between lenders and third-party settlement service agents in the real estate settlement process (Section 8 of RESPA). Even reciprocal referrals among these types of professions could be construed in court as a violation of the law of RESPA. It requires lenders to provide a good faith estimate for all the approximate costs of a particular loan and finally a HUD-1 (for purchase real estate loans) or a HUD-1A (for refinances of real estate loans) at the closing of the real estate loan. The final HUD-1 or HUD-1A allows the borrower to know specifically the costs of the loan and to whom the fees are being allotted. Beginning January 1, 2010, amendments to RESPA restrict the amount that fees can increase between the GFE and HUD-1 or HUD-1A. Origination charges are not allowed to increase, while certain third party service providers' fees can increase by no more than 10%.

If the borrower believes there is an error in the mortgage account, he or she can make a "qualified written request" to the loan servicer. The request must be in writing, identify the borrower by name and account, and include a statement of reasons why the borrower believes the account is in error. The request should include the words "qualified written request". It cannot be written on the payment coupon, but must be on a separate piece of paper. The Department of Housing and Urban Development provides a sample letter. The servicer must acknowledge receipt of the request within five business days. The servicer then has 30 business days (from the request) to take action on the request. The servicer has to either provide a written notification that the error has been corrected, or provide a written explanation as to why the servicer believes the account is correct. Either way, the servicer has to provide the name and telephone number of a person with whom the borrower can discuss the matter. The servicer cannot provide information to any credit agency regarding any overdue payment during the 60 day period. If the servicer fails to comply with the "qualified written request", the borrower is entitled to actual damages, up to $2,000 of additional damages if there is a pattern of noncompliance, costs and attorneys' fees.

Important issues concerning the loan to address are Robo Signers,

1. Improper Assignment Transfers,
2. Foreclosure Fraud,
3. Improper Mortgage Securitization -Separation of Promissory Note and Security Instrument, etc.

Step 7: Federal Foreclosure Complaints to Stop Foreclosure

It is really important to contact the correct government agencies and federal regulators to hold those who abuse state foreclosure laws accountable.

The most important government agencies to contact about problems with your mortgage loans are

1. Attorney General -For Your State,
2. U.S. Department of Justice,
3. Controller of Currency.

Step 8: Foreclosure Demand Letter to Stop Foreclosure

The same as with using a QWR a foreclosure demand letter can address issues and concerns about the mortgage loan. The foreclosure demand letter can be used to point out improper mortgage securitization issues why the lender lacks standing to foreclose on the property.

Step 9: Quite Title FREE and Clear Title

One of the best defenses against foreclosure is Quiet Title. A method used to clear clouds in the chain of title. Every state allows for Quiet Title Action. However, each state has Quiet Title guidelines designed for the specific state. Make sure that you follow Quiet Title guidelines by state correctly.

The purpose of Quiet Title is to Free and Clear clouds in the chain of title. Typically, the homeowner details why certain documents are improper and clouding the chain of title. A request is made to the court to clear the instruments that are improper in the chain of title so that they may be removed.

At any time a party may make claim to be a holder of a mortgage note. However, Quiet Title Action is designed to free and clear the chain of title.

Don't Believe the Hype

You may have heard from mainstream media reports that try to have you believe that the foreclosure crisis is over and the real estate markets are recovering. Nothing could be further from the truth. Our economy is worse than it was in the Great Depression. Millions of families have lost their home and many are homeless. The sad thing is that many of those people had their house stolen from them by a mortgage lender who foreclosed on their home without having the proper authority to do so. This is due to the fact that many homeowners did not challenge their mortgage lender when they receive the foreclosure notice. Please don't be another victim of wrongful foreclosure. When you receive a foreclosure notice you must and make your mortgage lender validate the debt.

More Resources

http://gofightforeclosure.com/2.0/

http://qwrattack.gofightforeclosure.com/

http://gofightforeclosure.com/2/

http://gofightforeclosure.com/blog/

www.ingramcontent.com/pod-product-compliance
Lightning Source LLC
Chambersburg PA
CBHW041610180526
45159CB00002BC/800